Amazing HOME SWEET HOME

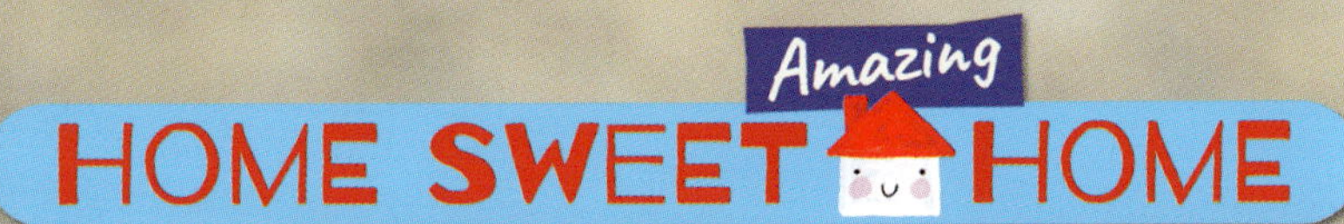

Hermit Crab's New Shell

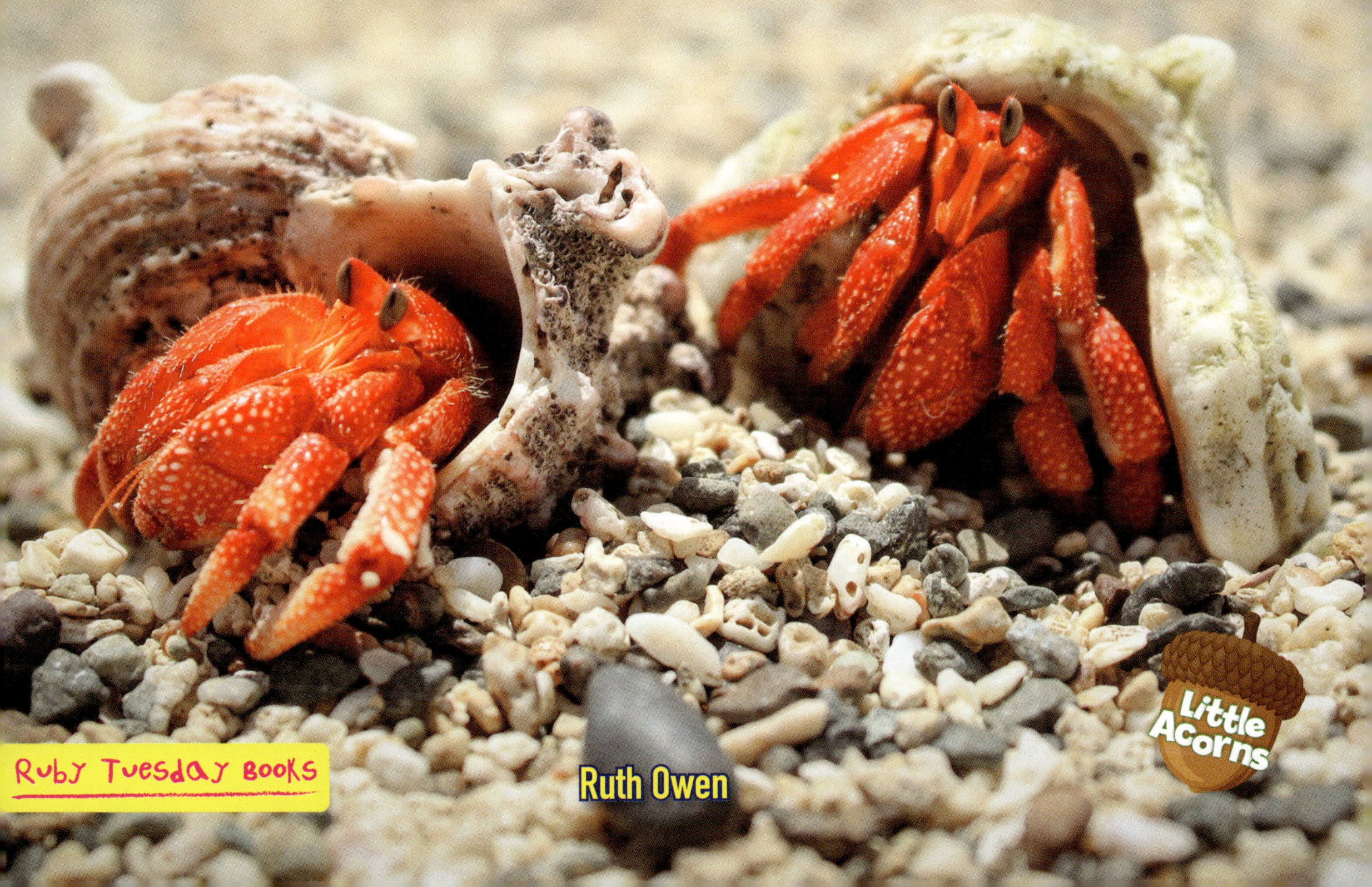

Ruby Tuesday Books

Ruth Owen

Little Acorns

Published in 2026 by Ruby Tuesday Books Ltd.

Editor: Mark J. Sachner
Design & Production: Tammy West

Photo Credits:
Alamy: Cover L (Minden Pictures), 4 (A&J Visage), 6B, 7TL, 22T (Biosphoto), 17 (cbimages), 18 (malvikabphotography); istockPhoto: 8, 9 (Sophie Dover); Nature Picture Library: 11 (Jane Burton), 12 (David Tipling), 13 (Javier Aznar), 14 (Georgette Douwma), 20 (Solvin Zankl); Science Photo Library: 10 (Georgette Douwma); Shutterstock: Cover R (Constantinos liopoulos), 1 (sagar__kumar), 2–3 (Le Panda/Green Art Story), 5, 6T, 7TR (fotogurmespb), 7BL (Samuel Kornstein), 7BR (Flystock), 8 (Mirelle), 15 (Vladimir Melnik/Wanida__Sri/MJ1995s/Wow Pho/Mark Brandon/Eric Isselee/Raymond Orton), 16 (kukiat B), 21 (Sakkarin Kamutsri), 22C (ViraVolg), 22B (sagar__kumar), 23T (Billion Photos), 23C (Fotowerkstatt__KS), 24 (Vladimir Melnik); Superstock: 19, 23B (D.P. Wilson/Minden Pictures).

Library of Congress Control Number: 2025946367

Print (Hardback) ISBN 978-1-78856-627-8
Print (Paperback) ISBN 978-1-78856-628-5
ePub ISBN 978-1-78856-629-2

Published in Minneapolis, MN
Printed in the United States

www.rubytuesdaybooks.com

CONTENTS

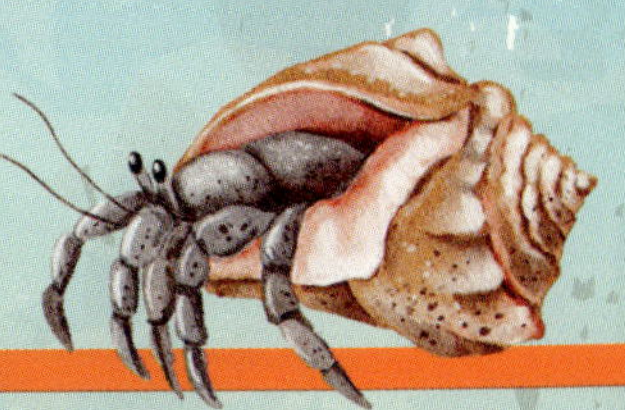

Too Tight!

It is early morning on a sandy beach.

A hermit crab is searching for food.

Hermit crabs eat dead fish, rotting seaweed, turtle eggs, and even poop.

But today, something is wrong.

The crab's shell feels **too tight!**

It is time to find a new, bigger protective home.

Most types of crabs have an **exoskeleton**, or shell, that covers their whole body.

A hermit crab does not have a shell on its soft **abdomen.**

Hard shell

Soft abdomen

Hard shell

How do hermit crabs protect their soft abdomens?

They wear a shell from another animal!

As a hermit crab grows bigger, its borrowed shell gets too small.

Hermit crabs use the shells of whelks, sea snails, and other shellfish.

It must search the beach for a bigger one.

Sometimes two hermit crabs want the same shell.

Then they fight using their big claws!

This hermit crab has found a dead sea snail. It eats the snail's body.

Then it moves into the snail's empty shell.

A hermit crab pulls its abdomen from its old, tight shell.

Then it slides its body into the new shell.

A hermit crab's shell keeps it safe.

If a hungry **predator** comes near, it tucks its body inside.

When a hermit crab swaps shells, it's a dangerous time!

A predator could grab its soft body.

Sometimes, a crab finds a shell that's just a little too big.

The crab waits, and soon other crabs gather.

Finally, a big crab arrives!

Now all the crabs form a line—from biggest to smallest.

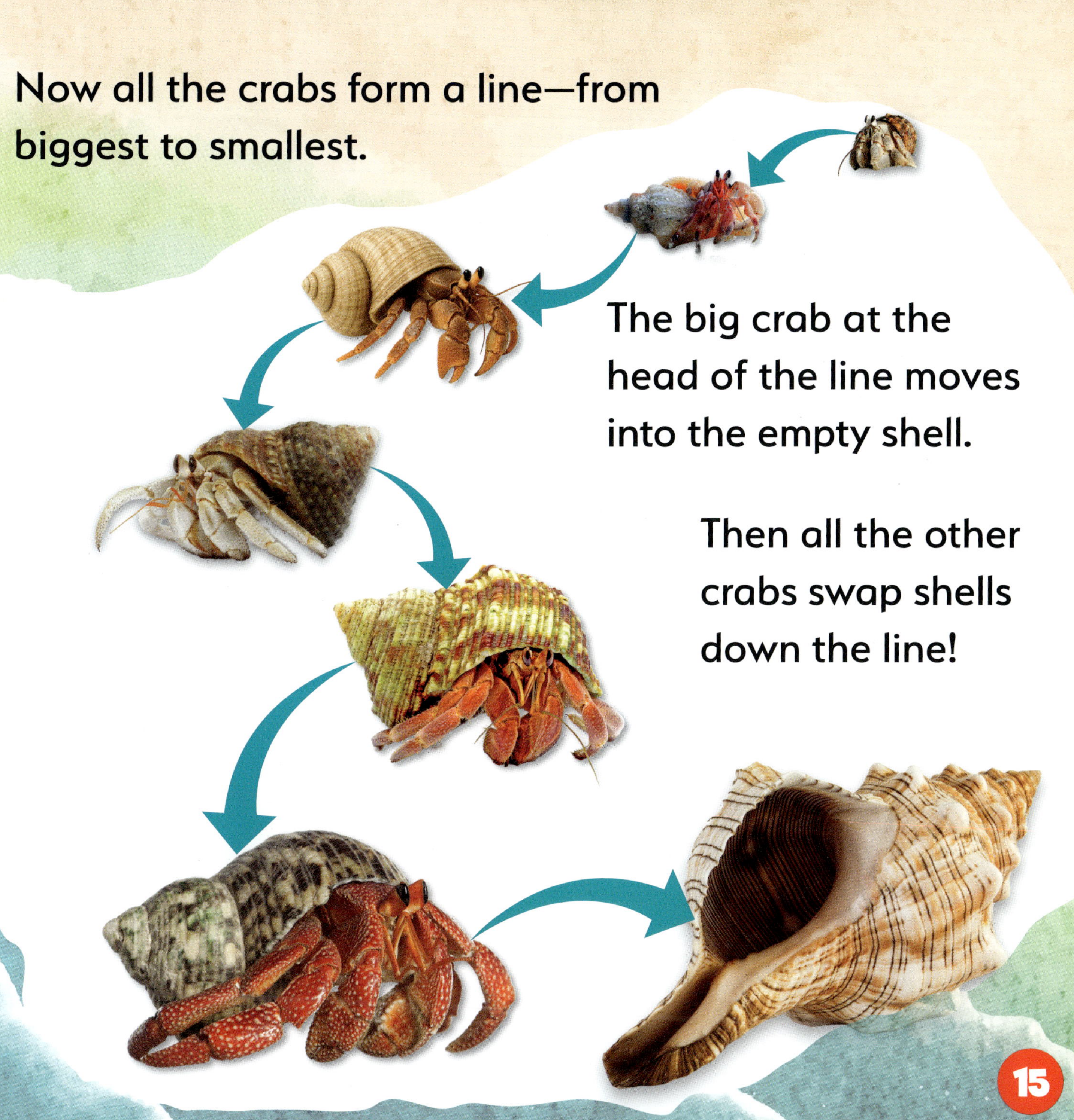

The big crab at the head of the line moves into the empty shell.

Then all the other crabs swap shells down the line!

There are about 1,000 different types of hermit crabs.

Some types spend their whole lives in the ocean.

Sometimes, clever hermit crabs turn trash into new homes!

You can see the crab's soft, curled abdomen inside its see-through, trash shell.

Male and female hermit crabs meet up to **mate.**

The female lays thousands of eggs!

She walks into the ocean to release her eggs into the water.

Baby crabs called **zoeas** hatch from the eggs.

The **microscopic** babies float in the ocean.

As a tiny zoea grows, its body and exoskeleton change shape.

After about 12 weeks, the little animal is ready to begin its life as a crab.

It finds a tiny shell to be its first amazing home!

Glossary

abdomen
The back part of a crab's body. Lobsters, shrimp, and animals such as spiders and insects also have a back part called an abdomen.

exoskeleton
A hard shell covering the body of some animals. Crabs, lobsters, spiders, and insects have an exoskeleton.

mate
To come together to produce young.

microscopic

Something so tiny it can only be seen with a microscope.

predator

An animal that hunts and eats other animals.

zoea

A microscopic baby hermit crab. Its name is pronounced "ZOH-ee-uh."

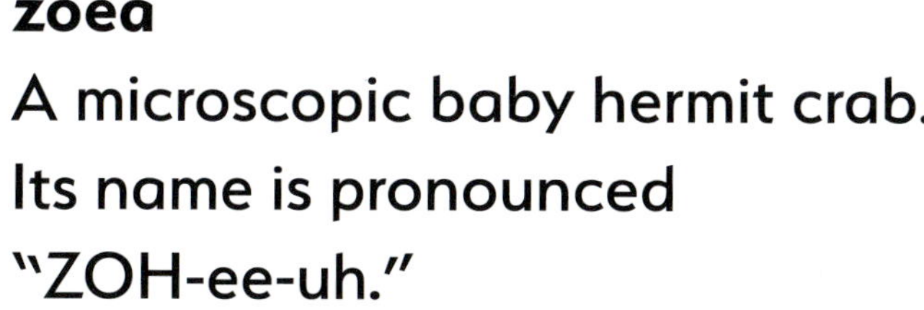

Index